# A LIFE FOR A LIFE?

PEACE·AND·JUSTICE·SERIES 9

# A LIFE FOR A LIFE?

## Death Penalty on Trial

## VERNON W. REDEKOP

HERALD PRESS
Scottdale, Pennsylvania
Waterloo, Ontario

**Library of Congress Cataloging-in-Publication Data**
Redekop, Vernon W., 1949-
    A life for a life : death penalty on trial / Vernon W.
Redekop.
        p. cm.
    ISBN 0-8361-3516-4 (alk. paper)
    1. Capital punishment—Religious aspects—Christianity.
I. Title.
HV8694.R42  1990
364.6'6—dc20                                          89-26709
                                                              CIP

The paper used in this publication meets the minimum requirements
of American National Standard for Information Sciences–Permanence
of Paper for Printed Library Materials, ANSI Z39.48-1984.

*To Gloria,*
*my lifelong companion in*
*the search for truth.*

# *Contents*

# Foreword

The problem of violent crime in North America is cause for grave concern. How should we as individuals and as a society respond to this problem? For many the answer lies in a "get tough" approach. They support longer or harsher prison sentences. They elect to carry handguns. And they advocate the use of the death penalty.

*A Life for a Life?* is a book for people of faith who look to their beliefs and to the Bible for guidance on personal and social morality. With a specific focus on the death penalty, author Vernon Redekop examines both the psychological mind-set and biblical justification that undergird so much of the support for state execution.

What does the Hebraic law actually say about the death penalty? When and why was it used in biblical accounts? How does our theological understanding of the life and teachings of Jesus inform us on this issue? What do the writings of Paul mean?

Going back to the original languages, the author does extensive translation and analysis to unlock the intention of biblical death penalty texts. For those who base their support for the death penalty on conventional interpretation of Scripture, Redekop raises some deep and disturbing questions.

But the author does not restrict himself to a narrow discussion of the death penalty. In Part Two he invites us to examine the principles that underlie our response to crime—not only to murder but to other crimes as well. He shares his conviction that society can develop creative and redemptive responses to the tragedy of violent crime.

In a thoughtful manner, Redekop enumerates elements which must be present if the victim, the offender, and the community are to move beyond anger, pain, and grief to healing and reconciliation. His book calls us to new personal and social responses. These must spring out of a holistic faith and a commitment to integrate that faith into even the most painful and harsh realities of life.

Redekop's book is a significant and timely contribution to our society's struggle with the problem of violent crime. First, because of his exacting research into the biblical teachings on the death penalty. Second, because he takes us beyond the death penalty debate to consider positive new directions for social responsibility.

> —*James V. Scott, Project Director*
> *Coalition Against the Return of the*
> *Death Penalty, Ottawa, Canada*

# *Acknowledgments*

The skills of Hebrew biblical analysis I learned from Professors Ken Berg, Allan Guenther, and particularly Elmer Martens at the Mennonite Brethren Biblical Seminary. Professor John E. Toews opened my eyes to a new understanding of biblical law. Jewish biblical scholars influenced my thinking through their writing.

My colleagues at the Church Council on Justice and Corrections stimulated my thinking on the connection between the Bible and criminal justice issues. To Lorraine Berzins, Dave McCord, James Scott, Jean Somers, and Lorraine Therriault, I am grateful.

Although they remain anonymous, the prisoners and victims who shared their stories with me have grounded this book in real life. Rae MacDonald suggested an entry for the first chapter.

Gloria Neufeld Redekop lent her considerable Greek exegetical skills to my analysis of New Testament texts. Her editorial assistance was also invaluable. Quinn, Natasha, and Lisa cheered me on to completion.

PART ONE

# The Death Penalty

# CHAPTER 1

# *Everybody Has Something to Say*

Recently two librarians were overheard discussing the death penalty. "Surely," urged one, "you wouldn't hesitate to execute someone who had murdered your child?"

"But what if it were *your* child I had to execute?" the other replied.

No matter what we do for a living, capital punishment involves us all. Like many similar questions, it tends to collect patterned responses. We've heard it discussed casually so often we may assume we've covered all the important points.

### What About You?

Certainly much has been said about the death penalty, but has the issue been made any clearer? Have you made up your mind? Do you believe some offenses are so grave that the offender should be put to death? What are these offenses? Can circumstances make a difference? Could you cast the deciding vote for execution if you had to rely on your feelings alone?

How important is it to you to know the answers to these questions? Do your answers involve your religious faith?

This book will assume that answers to these questions are important to you and others like you. You know that real people get killed by electric shock, hanging, injection, or firing squads; that real parents mourn the loss of a child who has been executed. You also understand that real victims suffer from the loss of spouse, children, and friends. They can spend years planning revenge.

This book also assumes that our decision about the death penalty involves religion on its various levels.

## A Religious Issue

Most churches have taken a stand on the death penalty. Some churches favor capital punishment. For example, the Fellowship of Evangelical Baptist Churches in Canada asked the Canadian government in 1985 to require the death penalty for first-degree murder.

On the other hand, many denominations oppose it. The Baptist Convention of Ontario and Quebec passed a resolution asking Canadian government for the continued abolition of capital punishment. (Canada abolished the death penalty for criminal offenses in 1976.)

Resolutions such as these by religious groups show that the death penalty is a religious issue. For men and women of Christian faith, a relationship with God is the foundation of life. It is therefore important that we know how God wants us to deal with those who do wrong within our justice system.

*A Personal Struggle*

Circumstances have forced me to deal with the death penalty question at a personal level. The story begins more than a decade ago when I left a teaching position in a tiny hamlet of Saskatchewan to direct a community center in downtown Montreal.

Upon my arrival there, I was asked to befriend a man serving a life sentence for killing his friend. The hundreds of hours I spent talking with "Harry" changed my view of the world. When he returned from the battlefields of Europe, he was devastated to find his children in an orphanage and his wife with a new mate. He began to deceive American tourists in Montreal bars. A girlfriend helped him crack open a safe.

As I listened, Harry went on to give the details that led to his killing his friend.

My abstract notion of crime changed during the four years I was intensely involved with prisoners. With this experience behind me, I went to seminary to reflect on all I had heard and seen. Learning Hebrew and Greek opened new understandings of biblical justice.

More recently I have shared deeply with victims of violent crime. Entering their experience of endless hurt and pain has directed me back to Scripture for new light on what to do about such crime.

In 1985 I was challenged to do a biblical study on capital punishment. Translating the death penalty teachings of the Old Testament from Hebrew to English was the first step. In some cases it took hours of research to unlock the full meaning of a single word. It was rewarding to discover insights I hadn't heard expressed before.

Later I was asked to prepare a death penalty statement for a church agency. As I developed the statement, I noticed that the Bible offers many positive responses to violent crime. In Part Two, I will explain the results of that study. But first we will examine what the Bible has to say about capital punishment.

## Questions for Reflection and Discussion

1. Why does crime—especially murder—often spark angry feelings and words from us?

2. Are criminals also people—persons who carry deep feelings of pain and loneliness? Should this make a difference in our response?

3. What do you think about capital punishment? Do you think Jesus would support its use?

# CHAPTER 2

# *Killing, You Shall Kill*

"If Clifford Olson [a serial murderer of children] were sitting in that electric chair, I'd run to push the button!" exclaimed a member of the Canadian Parliament at a televised debate on capital punishment.

"But *not* if he were your son," replied the journalist chairing the debate.

In a later debate the member of Parliament stated that if his own child were to be executed, he would do what he could to keep that child alive.

Joan Collins tells the story of her son Peter, who killed a police officer in 1983. Peter had repeated encounters with the police. His youthful defiance was answered harshly by the police. Each encounter intensified hatred and anger toward them. One summer day when under the influence of drugs, he acted out of anger.

After the police arrested him, they placed him in a maximum-security cell. Now his mother, who visits him regularly, sees his spirit softening. He is responding to her love. Her feelings about a possible execution are clear. Rather than running to push the button, she and her family would be devastated by such a loss.

How would you feel about executing your child, or a close friend who had done wrong? Would it surprise you that the most emphatic biblical teaching on capital punishment suggests family executions?

As you read the following text, remember that the Hebrew language used repetition to emphasize a point.

FURTHERMORE, suppose one of the following tries to turn you away from the LORD:

Your brother, the child of your mother,
Your son,
Your daughter,
Your wife who is close to you,
Your intimate friend who is like a part of you,

Saying, "Let us go and serve other gods
Which you yourself have not known
Nor your ancestors—
Some of the gods of the people who surround
  you,
The ones who are close to you
Or the ones who are far away from you,
From one end of the land to the other."

No way are you to consent to them.
No way are you to listen to them.
No way are you to look on them
  with compassion.
No way are you to spare them.
No way are you to hide them.

RATHER, *killing*, you shall *kill* them.
Your hand shall be the first upon them to *cause*
    them to *die*
And the hand of the people afterward.
You shall *stone* them with stones.
And they shall *die*.

FOR their desire has been to cause you to put
    aside
The LORD your God,
The One who caused you to leave the land
    of Egypt
Out of the house of slavery.
And all Israel shall hear of it and shall fear.
No way will they add on to this
By doing anything as wicked as this among you.
                                   —Deuteronomy 13:7-12
                                   (author's translation)

I know of no one who has obeyed this teaching.
Perhaps it was never intended to be taken literally.
This passage shows how easily relationships can be
destroyed. Pull the right thread and the whole
community can come apart. Start a destructive idea
with the wrong person and through friendships and
families it will permeate the whole community.

Consider the spread of drug abuse in society.
Imagine a small town where the people had lived a
quiet, peaceful life for years. All the members
knew one another. Most were related to others in
the town. One day someone traveled to the city
and experienced a high on cocaine. He brought
some back and introduced it to to his friends. They
shared it with their younger brothers and sisters
who took it into their schools. A businessperson
tried it and decided to sell it. Before long much of

the town was inhaling cocaine and the fabric of the community started to fall apart.

How would you deal with a close friend who was peddling drugs? Would you turn him or her in to the police? Such action would put you in a terrible bind.

This is the point of this biblical text. With great irony the strongest capital punishment teaching is reserved for situations in which people could never bring themselves to perform the execution. But it strengthens the primary teaching to love the Lord with all your heart, soul, strength, and mind.

The people of ancient Israel were as vulnerable to idols as we are to drugs. Idols were appealing. Because they were visible, they thereby provided a false security. Deuteronomy points out that intervention at the first sign of turning away from God was necessary.

The writer pleads desperately for Israel to stop the spread of evil. The struggle against evil is not primarily with exterior political threats. It is close to home. The message to every citizen is not to succumb to the pressure of idolatry even if it comes from a close friend.

Thus, this passage does not suggest killing on a large scale. Rather it warns the community against potential danger. It calls the community to prevent evil before it has a chance to destroy persons, and in the end, the community itself.

## Questions for Reflection and Discussion

1. Do you think you could stone your child (or pull the switch on the electric chair) if he or she were guilty of murder? Should your feelings make a

difference? Why or why not?

2. Why was the death penalty given in Deuteronomy 13:7-12 if it was so seldom carried out in Israel's history?

3. What do we value more than anything? What could destroy this value in the community?

# CHAPTER 3

# *Death-Deserving Behaviors*

It could be argued that the ancient Israelites accepted capital punishment for the following offenses: (1) shopping on the Lord's day, (2) cursing God, (3) cheating on income tax, and (4) having sexual intercourse with someone of another religion.

These offenses represent the four isolated cases of capital punishment in ancient Israel. However, only three executions are recorded in the first five books of the Bible and one in the sixth. These are the cases in which the community killed an individual in the face of wrongdoing.

Gathering wood on the Sabbath led to the first stoning. This could be compared to working or shopping on the Lord's day (Numbers 15:32-36).

Second, a man of half-Egyptian blood was stoned for cursing God in the middle of a fight with an Israelite (Leviticus 24:10-16).

Third, Aachan stole some goods from the city of Jericho after the walls came tumbling down. It was as though he took for himself something which belonged rightfully to the whole community. This is similar to cheating on income tax (Joshua 7:1-26).

Fourth, a man caught in bed with a woman who did not worship the God of the Israelites was speared to death (Numbers 25:1-9).

To say that the Israelites favored the death penalty is beside the point. In the cases of biblical executions, God made the decision to have them killed. In two cases Moses slept on the decision and God revealed to him that the executions were to take place. In the case of Aachan, who stole some property, lots were used to determine his guilt.

In the case of sleeping with the wrong person, the execution by javelin doesn't fit into the deliberate, planned taking of life by the community. Since the story is told as though the executioner did the right thing for the community, it may be included in our study. In all four cases, the story is told to show God desired the execution.

In the three cases of stoning, the executioners left behind a pile of stones as a reminder of the occasion. Because each was for a different offense, the people could point to the cairn and tell their children, "Under this pile of stones is the body of a person who. . . ." With that introduction the entire story of a particular event would unfold.

These executions, all for religious offenses, happened at critical times. If left unchecked, the offenses might have disrupted the whole community. For example, the man who gathered wood did it on the Sabbath, just when the idea of resting on the Lord's day was being established legally. Since wood in the wilderness was scarce, this put him at an unfair advantage over everyone else. Had he been permitted to do so, community discipline on the Sabbath (which was hard to maintain in the best of times) might have broken down. Keeping the Sabbath was one of the most significant actions for the identity of the Jewish community.

The half-Egyptian who cursed God in the middle of a fight threatened the faith of the whole community, for belief in God was quite fragile. Had he been able to defy God and get away with it, even win the fight, the people's faith would have been weakened. Because the Israelites were used to taking orders from their Egyptian masters, this man might have been able to gain quite a following among the people.

When Aachan stole property from Jericho, his example was important, for this was the first city of Canaan to be handed over to the Israelites. Had there been wholesale looting of the cities, it would have led to rivalry and conflict over possessions. All the goods in the city were to be put in the treasury of the Lord their God. Aachan stole from God and in doing so broke the covenant between God and the community.

In the case of the clan *leader* sleeping with a woman of another faith, this activity united him with someone who gave allegiance to idols. Had it become widespread the people might have lost their devotion to God.

### Death Penalty Teachings

Many other behaviors were associated with death in the Old Testament even though there is no record of executions for these activities. Just as good behavior offered life and power to people, evil was associated with curses and death. Both death and curses limited their life choices.

Each of the behaviors listed below opened the community to danger. If these activities had become widespread (as they did at certain times), Israel's relationship with God would have changed greatly. The covenant community may have been destroyed.

Adam and Eve were told that if they ate the fruit of a certain tree, *dying, they would die*. (This is the form used in most death penalty teachings.) They ate of the fruit and their lives changed. They were cursed (limited in their choices). Afterward, they had to work hard and endure hardship outside the garden.

As you read the list below, think about how each of these might distract from the goal of the community: to sustain a relationship with a creating, life-oriented God.

## Religious Acts Associated with Death

1. Eating the fruit of the tree of the knowledge of good and evil in the garden. (Genesis 2:17)

2. Touching Mount Sinai while God was giving the Ten Commandments. (Exodus 19:12)

3. Practicing sorcery. (Leviticus 20:27; Exodus 22:17)

4. Sacrificing to another god. (Exodus 22:30)

5. Not keeping the Sabbath. (Exodus 31:14-15)

6. Sacrificing children to Molech, a Canaanite god. (Leviticus 20:2)

7. Cursing God. (Leviticus 24:10-16)

8. Going too close to the sacred tent, altar, or ark. (Numbers 1:51; 3:10, 38; 18:7)

9. Being a false prophet. (Deuteronomy 13:5)

10. Worshiping idols. (Deuteronomy 13:16; 17:2-5; Exodus 22:20)

11. Getting a friend, parent, or child to worship another god. (Deuteronomy 13:7-12)

### Rebellious Acts Associated with Death

12. Assaulting one's father or mother. (Exodus 21:15)

13. Cursing one's parents. (Exodus 21:17; Leviticus 20:9)

14. Rebelling against leaders. (Deuteronomy 17:12; Joshua 1:18; Numbers 16; Exodus 22:27)

15. Rebelling against parents. (Deuteronomy 21:21)

### Sexual Acts Associated with Death

16. Having intercourse with beasts. (Leviticus 22:19; Leviticus 20:15-16)

17. Committing adultery. (Leviticus 20:10)

18. Having intercourse with one's father's wife. (Leviticus 20:11)

19. Having intercourse with one's daughter-in-law. (Leviticus 20:12)

20. Having intercourse with another man. (Leviticus 20:13)

21. Having intercourse with one's mother-in-law. (Leviticus 20:14)

22. Becoming a prostitute, if the daughter of a priest. (Leviticus 21:9)

23. Being found not a virgin at the time of marriage. (Deuteronomy 22:20)

24. Raping or consenting to rape. (Deuteronomy 22:24-26)

*Hurtful Acts Associated with Death*
25. Kidnapping. (Exodus 21:16; Deuteronomy 24:7)
26. Keeping a dangerous ox. (Exodus 21:28-32)
27. Oppressing refugees or people on welfare (widows and orphans). (Exodus 22:23)
28. Murdering. (Genesis 9:6; Exodus 21:12; Leviticus 24:16-21; Numbers 35:16-39; Deuteronomy 19:6)
29. Being a false witness for any of the above. (Deuteronomy 19:16-19)

Many Old Testament leaders engaged in some of these behaviors. Of the 12 sons of Jacob, all but Joseph, Benjamin, and Reuben were kidnappers. Judah, the patriarch, was guilty of intercourse with his daughter-in-law. Reuben slept with his father's wife. Moses was a murderer. King David was both a murderer and an adulterer.

All of these offenders suffered in some way. Moses had to spend time in the wilderness and David's family was plagued with serious conflict. Reuben lost his privileges as the oldest son.

Cain, the first murderer, could no longer stay on his own farm but was driven to a life of wandering. This limitation on his life was more than he could bear, for he was a farmer at heart. Although God protected Cain's life, Cain lost a sense of rootedness. His offspring became the first city dwellers.

According to the prophets' interpretation of history, widespread engagement in these forbidden activities led to the demise of the Northern Kingdom of Israel. And a combination of idolatry, adultery, and economic exploitation of the poor led the Southern Kingdom (Judah) into exile for 70 years.

Although the list of acts associated with death is long, the actual use of the death penalty in the Bible was limited. In the few situations in which God made it clear that individuals were to be executed, the community was in special danger.

Since the Bible tells a story which continues through centuries, it is possible to see the long-term consequences of these behaviors associated with death. For the community of faith, the story helps to reinforce the positive values needed to sustain a good life for everyone.

Let us now look at murder in the Bible.

## Questions for Reflection and Discussion

1. What observations can you make from this survey of Old Testament teaching and practice?

2. Many Old Testament heroes committed criminal acts. What were the consequences?

3. Why were only several cases of the death penalty recorded in the Bible?

CHAPTER 4

# Cold-Blooded Murder

When I began this study of the Hebrew Scriptures several years ago, I went out for coffee with a young minister. He understood Genesis 9:6 to be a universal, timeless principle: "Man was made like God, so whoever murders a man will himself be killed by his fellowman." Isn't this text clear as normally translated? Murder for murder.

This text comes right after the story of Noah. The people's sin was so great that God wiped out humanity through the Flood. Then God promised never again to destroy all the people on the earth.

Genesis 9:6 is poetry, more like a proverb than a law. Through it God was lecturing Noah on the value of life. I noticed the word *Adam* (humankind) occurs three times. My translation is:

> The one shedding blood of humankind—
> In humankind will his own blood be shed.
> FOR in the image of God
> Was humankind made.

It suggests to me two interpretations:

First, God identifies with humankind as a whole. Therefore, those who take life away from the human community are taking life away from themselves. According to Genesis 1, God made humankind (male and female) in his own image. It is humankind as a whole which reflects God's image in this world, making us part of one another. To kill any individual therefore destroys part of our common life. Tribal communities understand this better than cultures which emphasize individuality.

Second, if anyone attempts to take away the life of the entire community in a manner similar to the Flood, that person will be destroying himself or herself. Since our lives have meaning in community, to wipe out part of the human community is to destroy ourselves.

The text makes the point that the life of the human community is of great importance to God.

### A Story of Murder

Since the Old Testament does not record an execution for murder, let's create the type of situation to which the teachings about murder might apply.

Abseh had a sheep ranch, while Benshor raised cattle on the hills of Ephraim. Each owned territory, marked by some distinctive stones. From time to time Abseh's sheep wandered across the border and grazed the grass to the ground. The shepherds looked the other way when this happened. Benshor complained to Abseh. Soon after, Benshor noticed the stones were being moved. He tried to move them back but the next morning they were farther onto his property.

As this continued, Benshor, who had fewer servants to tend his small herd of cattle, felt increasingly powerless and angry. One day he was out inspecting his pastures when he saw Abseh on the other side of the boundary markers checking out his grass. This was the occasion he had been waiting for. He gave Abseh a friendly greeting and walked up to him. When they were close, he pulled out a knife and stabbed his neighbor to death.

Now Go'el Haddam (literally redeemer of the blood) comes upon the scene. He was the older brother of Abseh and the next of kin. He became very angry about the loss of his brother, both because he loved his brother and because his clan had lost a strong and prosperous member. He now had to look after Abseh's widow and children.

Since he did not live close by, it would be quite a hardship. He could sell the land and sheep and take in the widow, but who would buy the land? If he was not vigilant, Benshor would take over a good bit of it. The way for him to look after his clan's interests, he figured, was to kill Benshor in revenge. He started to make these plans soon after the murder.

When Benshor realized that Go'el was after him, he ran to the nearest city of refuge and clung to the horns of the altar. This was the sacred place where no one could touch him. If he was not convicted of planning the murder he would have to stay in the city of refuge until the local priest died. Then he would be free to go back to the ranch. If he wandered out of the city and Go'el found him, Go'el could kill him without getting into trouble.

The murderer was tried before a group of elders. Two witnesses to the murder, however, were necessary to convict Benshor and have him handed over to Go'el.

## Implications

This story summarizes the biblical teaching on murder. Most of the teaching concerns itself with limiting vengeance. It makes provision for cities of refuge and a trial (see Joshua 20:2-6). It was not the community which executed the murderer, but rather the victim's next of kin.

The story also illustrates the cycle of injustice and violence which can easily increase. Benshor was motivated by hatred to kill Abseh. That hatred was nurtured by the injustices Abseh did to Benshor. Benshor was the victim, but became the offender. At that point Go'el was motivated by anger and hatred to kill Benshor. Had there been no controls, he might have killed not only Benshor, but also members of Benshor's family. Then a feud would have followed.

The Jewish tradition gives us details about how this case would have been handled. The trial would occur in front of 23 judges. At least 13 of them would have to agree that it was in fact first-degree murder. Only 12 would be needed for acquittal.

For conviction, the law required the testimony of two witnesses. Both of them had to have seen the entire crime. It was not enough for them to have seen Benshor with a bloody knife and Abseh lying on the ground. They had to agree on every detail about when, where, and how it happened. The witnesses could change their mind in favor of details leading to acquittal, but they could not change information in favor of details which might lead to conviction.

If the beginning testimony made it look as though revenge were justified, and later one of the witnesses changed testimony, the offender could not be killed. If at any point the witnesses disagreed, the offender could not be killed, for no further change of testimony would be allowed.

In the application of this law, therefore, all the procedures were stacked *in favor of the accused.* Any real application of the death penalty on the basis of biblical teaching was virtually ruled out. Jewish literature supports this conclusion. A court which executed one person in 70 years was considered a destructive one.

Biblical teaching is realistic in acknowledging feelings of vengeance after a murder. The role of the community is to protect the accused from a quick execution and to provide a safe place to live while it is all worked out.

The biblical teaching we noted in chapter 2 emphasized the command to kill the friend or relative to safeguard the community. Here, however, the emphasis falls on limiting the speedy taking of life to avenge a murder.

## Jewish Interpretation

The Jewish community interpreted the Bible according to the principle of *mercy.* Certain texts allowed for certain actions, but one had to attempt to go beyond the precise requirements of the Torah in the direction of love and mercy. To do so was to live the Torah.

For example, divorce was allowed in certain cases. This did not mean that one had to divorce an unfaithful partner. If one was able to love and forgive, this was so much better. Think about the following text which comes out of a Jewish writing near the time of Jesus.

> Beware, my children, of those who hate, because it leads to lawlessness against the Lord himself. Hatred does not want to hear repeated his commands concerning love of neighbors, and thus it sins against God. For if a brother makes a false step, immediately it wants to spread the tale to everyone, and is eager to have him condemned for it, punished and executed. . . . *Just as love wants to bring the dead back to life and to recall those under sentence of death, so hate wants to kill the living and does not wish to preserve alive those who have committed the slightest sin.*
>
> For among all men the spirit of hatred works by Satan through human frailty for the death of mankind; but the spirit of love works by the Law of God through forbearance for the salvation of mankind. (Testament of Gad 4:1-7)
> —From Charlesworth, James H., editor, *The Old Testament Pseudepigrapha*, Garden City, N.Y.: Doubleday, 1983, p. 815.

We have studied the fictional story of Abseh and Benshor in the light of biblical teaching on murder. We have seen that in ancient Israel the emphasis was on limiting revenge killing. In the case of deliberate murder, allowance was made in biblical teaching for revenge to occur after a trial. But we know from Jewish sources that the trial procedure was aimed at making vengeance killing almost impossible.

Genesis 9:6 makes clear that all human life is precious and that we hurt ourselves if we "shed the blood" of another person. As we deal with biblical teaching, it becomes important that we interpret it in a spirit of mercy. We can use a text to give license to hate or to express love. The apostle Paul noted that "all things are lawful . . . but not all things are helpful" (1 Corinthians 6:12).

We have to decide how to interpret these texts. In our interpretation we must struggle to come to terms with the whole message of the Bible.

## Questions for Reflection and Discussion

1. The Bible admits that angry feelings normally follow murder. What important role did the community play with regard to feelings of vengeance?

2. With what spirit should we interpret the Scripture?

3. What role did mercy play in these Old Testament texts?

# CHAPTER 5

# *Vengeance Is Mine*

The owner of a pharmacy in Calgary, Alberta, shot and killed a man robbing his store. Immediately other business people raised thousands of dollars to help him with his legal fees.

Bernard Goetz in New York City received wide public support after shooting some black youths who attacked him in a subway. He was acquitted of the main charges against him and became something of a folk hero.

Why do so many people cheer inwardly in the face of violent revenge? We have become accustomed to think of justice as "just punishment" or "getting the punishment one deserves."

The real equation in North America seems to be: JUSTICE = PUNISHMENT = REVENGE.

It is played out on television every night. We cheer when the "bad guy" is hurt or "equalized."

However, this does not square with the biblical concept of justice which emphasizes making relationships right. The word often translated *righteous* comes from the word for justice. This distinction does not satisfy those angry people who wish to see offenders punished rather than restored to wholeness in the community.

The biblical word, "Vengeance is *mine*; I will repay, says the Lord," could be read, "Punishment is for me; I will do the punishing, says the Lord."

How does the Lord deal with the desire to punish, a desire born of deep sustained anger? To answer, we will look first at the dynamics of anger and then at how God handled anger.

Jason grew up on a reserve near Brandon, Manitoba. At the age of eight he was taken away from his mother, who had an alcohol problem. Since he loved his mother, it hurt him deeply to leave her. After being shunted from one foster home to another, a man living in Kansas finally adopted him. It appeared to be a good arrangement. The man was a respected member of the community with a good job and financial security.

Behind closed doors, however, there was repeated sexual abuse. Jason tried to run away but he was always caught. Through the years his anger built up. He was trapped, abused with no way out. Finally, he brutally killed his adopted father.

Anger is an emotion known to all of us. We all have triggers which ignite bursts of temper. We also experience the slow buildup of frustration over time. Finally, the resulting anger erupts in strong impulsive action.

When we are angry we are most vulnerable to the power of evil. We are most likely to do something hurtful. That's why the teaching to "love one's neighbor as one's self" is given in the context of anger control (Leviticus 19:17-18).

The Bible acknowledges the emotion of anger, both by God and by human beings. Early in the history of Israel, the whole community got carried away with death-deserving behavior twice. God was angry enough to have them "killed as one person" (Numbers 14:15)—to execute the whole community. On both occasions God wanted to start all over with Moses. And on both occasions Moses argued with God in prayer:

> LORD, O LORD God,
> Compassionate and generous with your favor,
> Slow to anger and great in merciful love and
>     faithfulness,
> Demonstrating merciful love to the clans,
> Forgiving guilt and the sin of revolt and
>     terrible wrongdoing,
> And cleansing them from the need for punishment.
> This cleansing is not absolute
> Since the consequences of the parents' sin will
>     affect
> Children and grandchildren to the fourth
>     generation.
>
> —Exodus 34:6-7 and Numbers 14:15
> (author's translation)

God was persuaded and spared the people. But we are not God. Does that mean we can do as we like—that we can kill those who make us angry? Isn't that what capital punishment is all about?

Our anger is frequently aroused when we experience the opposite of our deepest values. Some of us get angry when we think of Clifford Olson, a Canadian who killed 11 young people. Others get angry when someone who has committed rape is acquitted because a fine point of the law was not followed.

In these two cases, we rightly value children living out their lives without being raped or killed, and we rightly value people being held accountable for their actions. One person told me that if the death penalty should be used for anything, it should be for income-tax evasion by the rich. By this action they were increasing the burden for the poor. Such cheating arouses his anger.

Our desire for punishment is motivated by anger. Much of popular culture supports the violent expression of anger by "good guys" against the "bad guys."

"Vengeance is *mine*" really means, "Express your anger to me and leave it at that." The Bible has more to say on the subject and we will examine more of the biblical material in chapter 11. But first we will deal with the death penalty and compare it with the character of Jesus.

### Questions for Reflection and Discussion

1. What is the biblical concept of justice? To what extent does it match typical understandings of justice in the United States and Canada?

2. Is it wrong to be angry? Why or why not?

3. When are we most capable of doing evil?

# CHAPTER 6
# *Child of . . .*

The Qumran community which was active at the time of Jesus separated the world into "children of light" and "children of darkness." The former lived uprightly, the latter were evil.

Those who wish to pattern their lives after Jesus, the "Son of God," ought to ask what "Son of God" meant to Jesus. Certainly a unique relationship was involved, but the strong link between "child of" and character is usually lost.

By describing himself as the "Son of God," Jesus was saying that his actions, character, and *mission* were those of God.

When Jesus invited people to become disciples or "children of God," he invited them to live as he lived. That is why he repeatedly asked people to believe in him. If they couldn't, they should at least believe in his *actions* (John 10:37-38). He challenged his audience to examine critically his actions to see if they produced good fruit. His question was in effect, "Are the lives of people better or worse because of what I am doing?"

At one point his contemporaries claimed to be children of Abraham. Jesus replied that they were not Abraham's children because they did not act like Abraham (John 8:39-44). Rather, he said, they were children of the devil because they were acting as the devil acted. *Actions* associated with the devil are murdering and lying.

The sum of Jesus' actions was evident in his *character.* His reputation reflected what people understood of this character. They knew him for his healing and his association with the outcasts of society—the "publicans, sinners, and prostitutes."

He had a *mission* to "do the will of God." To act like God, who was "slow to anger and great in merciful love," sometimes brought joy and sometimes pain.

Jesus' *mission* clearly was not to condemn people. He was not out to judge and punish. People of the world were already suffering from the ill effects of their hurtful acts. What they needed was relief from the vicious cycles of wrongdoing.

*Salvation* in the Bible means deliverance and blessing. For Jesus, saving people from their sins meant helping them out of a behavior pattern which was destroying them and the people around them. Such deliverance also brought the blessings of safety and good relationships.

As he healed people of their diseases and demons, Jesus brought new hope and new life. This work was not without pain. Jesus grieved at the death of Lazarus (John 11:35). He moaned all the way to the tomb (John 11:38). At other times he was tired. On occasion he resisted a call for help. His reward was the joy on the faces of the sick and the rejected as they discovered relief and acceptance.

At the annual meeting of the Canadian Church Press a few years ago, I talked about the death penalty with one of Canada's leaders within the evangelical church community. His reading of the New Testament convinced him to oppose capital punishment, for every time he found an urge to kill, it was associated with demons. The ministry of Jesus, he found, was always associated with the giving of life. Furthermore, he found that no individual was beyond hope. He saw, therefore, that the urge to have the state take a person's life could not be motivated by the Spirit of Jesus.

In effect, he was arguing that a death penalty position could not be based on the life and teaching of Jesus. The idea could more easily be associated with the work of the devil.

We know that the children of abusive parents often become abusers themselves. Their children can eventually themselves become abusers. This cycle is hard to break. The victim takes out his or her hurt and anger on another generation. Children of hurt produce hurt. It is the fruit of the behavior.

Salvation means that the cycle can be broken. Our children do not have to continue the sins of their parents.

We frequently use the phrase "child of . . ." or "son of . . ." to mean that the person had the actions, character, and mission of the parent. Jesus, as the Son of God, reflected the traits of God as revealed in the Old Testament. Reading accounts of Jesus' life we find that his mission and character were not caught up in punishing people. Rather,

Jesus offered salvation from the vicious cycle of sin.

Although the children of abusers and of criminals have a greater tendency to be abusers and criminals themselves, this need not be the case. The hope of salvation can change them.

We have begun to probe on three levels the concept of being a "child of something" regarding the death penalty:

1. Jesus as the Son of God exemplified the mercy of God.

2. The urge to kill in revenge can be thought of as the child of someone. Who is the more likely parent?

3. Children of abusers often carry on the behaviors of their parents but the cycle can be stopped. People can be saved from their own impulses.

We turn now to the *teachings* of Jesus for more insight.

## Questions for Reflection and Discussion

1. What traits of your parents do you see in yourself?

2. Can you think of any common "child of . . ." or "son of . . ." phrases that are meant to portray someone's character?

3. What difference does it make if the urge to kill comes from the devil?

# CHAPTER 7

# *The Teachings of Jesus*

A man in Montreal owned many apartment blocks in a poor area of the city. He borrowed heavily to acquire more property. When interest rates rose and property values fell, he was about to lose everything. Since he was an older man, he had little chance of rebuilding a business or finding employment.

Although in debt several hundred thousand dollars, his creditors, who had known him for a long time, decided to give him a break. They put off any payments or interest charges until his financial situation changed.

In one of the man's apartments lived a woman with three children who had only a low-paying job. Her rent took a major part of her income. One of her children became critically ill, and she had to stay home for several weeks. She lost her job. As a result, she simply could not pay the rent for a couple of months.

The landlord went to see her to demand payment. When she couldn't pay, he ordered her to move out. She protested that she would pay when her child was well and she could work again, but that was not good enough.

When the creditors heard the story, they called the man to account. They decided to treat him as he had treated the woman who owed him several hundred dollars. They demanded that he pay his debts immediately. He went bankrupt and lost everything.

This modern-day version of one of Jesus' parables illustrates how the way we treat others shapes the way we are treated.

The teachings of Jesus are practical: When sued, settle privately before getting to court. Judge not that you be not judged. Do to others as you would have them do to you. Forgive debts so you will be forgiven the debts you can't pay.

This connection between our actions and how we are treated raises some questions, though. If Jesus is advocating that we be treated as we treat others, does that include rape, assault, and murder? Should we rape the rapists, assault the violent, and kill the murderers? Is this vengeance on the part of Jesus?

To what extent does our behavior affect how we are treated now and to what degree do we await final judgment before God? Jesus taught that those who are good to the naked and the poor have been good to him and are to be rewarded at the final judgment. Even those who may have been pious but who neglected the needy are to be punished.

As I reflected on these teachings of Jesus, I asked myself, "What point is he making?" It seems that Jesus' emphasis falls on our behavior. He wants us to become less judgmental, more merciful, less hypocritical, and more concerned with the pain of the hurting. He is trying to motivate moral growth by pointing out the consequences of our actions. He is saying, "Don't be short-sighted. The results of your actions go on and on. Your actions are remembered by people and by God. When decisions are to be made about you, the memories of what you have done will affect those decisions."

When Jesus talks about how we should respond to wrongdoing against us, his focus is different. He does not say, "If someone slaps you, your response should be linked to his action. So hit him back." Rather, Jesus teaches that we turn the other cheek. Similarly we should go beyond the call of duty in helping others who force us to serve them. Jesus actually states that we should love our enemies and be prepared to die even for an evil person.

See the distinction? When we are thinking of being nasty to someone, Jesus says, "Hold on. Do you know what you are doing? The reality is that you could be asking for trouble." When someone is being nasty to us, Jesus says, "I am introducing a new kingdom with a new standard of behavior. Rather than seeking revenge, decide to do something good. Be creative."

We must also consider the teachings of Jesus about the sinner or serious criminal. The parables of the lost sheep, the lost son, and the lost coin point to one truth. There is great celebration in the kingdom of God when someone whom the community has rejected is restored to full membership.

Jesus was constantly befriending and helping the outcasts of his time. Sinners, lepers, and tax collectors were "unclean." They were set apart from the rest of society. One was not to associate with them, let alone have a meal with them. Yet Jesus did it again and again. He did not suggest that the sinners and tax collectors be treated as they had treated others. When Jesus befriended tax collector Zacchaeus, the man responded by returning four-fold any money he had wrongfully collected.

In relating Jesus' teaching to the death penalty, remember that those executed are often from the weakest communities in society. They tend to be poor, black, Native American, or a member of a visible minority group. Jesus made a special point of befriending persons from minority groups unpopular within the dominant culture.

Jesus himself was executed. His death has been a primary focus in Christianity. The cross was the ancient symbol of capital punishment. It has become the symbol of Christianity.

## Questions for Reflection and Discussion

1. What new standard of behavior did Jesus introduce?

2. By what standard will God judge us?

3. What about grace through faith? Will God actually pay attention to our behavior in the final judgment?

# CHAPTER 8

# *The Meaning of Jesus' Death*

Jesus was crucified by the government of Rome on the grounds that he was a threat to society. I have already pointed out that the Jewish people were extremely reluctant to impose capital punishment. Many procedures made it virtually impossible to convict anyone.

The Jews of Palestine did not have the power to impose the death penalty even if they wanted to. Historians think a certain amount of stoning went on anyhow, and the Romans simply looked the other way—as long as the general populace remained calm.

When the adulteress about to be stoned was brought to Jesus, they wanted to test Jesus on his interpretation of the law (John 8:1-11). Would he demand death when they could not legally stone her under Roman law? By writing in the sand, Jesus may have spelled out the regulations for the special Jewish courts to handle capital offenses. It was obvious that these had not been fulfilled.

Jesus then said, "Would the one who has not

sinned throw the first stone." The woman's accusers wanted to execute her without Roman consent, knowing they would get away with it. Jesus showed that the death penalty of the Old Testament was intended to encourage moral behavior.

On several occasions they tried the same trick on Jesus. They tried to prove he was either mad—filled with an evil spirit (John 8:4-8; 10:19-33)—blasphemous, or a false prophet (John 7:52). Any of these would qualify as a capital offense under Jewish law. (See the list on pages 27-29.) Some then tried to stone him, but Jesus successfully eluded them. As his popularity grew, the people around him served to protect him.

A small group of political leaders then conspired to have the Romans execute Jesus. They controlled the business enterprises of the temple and were making a healthy profit by selling animals for sacrifice. Jesus had attacked this practice, undermining their authority. When Jesus taught against love of money, these people laughed at him. Finally, they persuaded the treasurer of Jesus' company to join their cause.

At this point Jesus could have dismissed Judas and escaped from Jerusalem to avoid execution. He chose not to run. Neither did he summon supernatural forces to protect him.

The small group of political leaders who talked the Romans into crucifying Jesus were the Sadducees and a few of the Pharisees. As they discussed Jesus in the ruling Sanhedrin, some of the Pharisees spoke up on his behalf. (Nicodemus and Joseph of Arimathea were both leading Pharisees who believed in Jesus.)

This is not surprising since many of Jesus' teachings were identical to those of Hillel, a famous rabbi of his time. Hillel, a Pharisee, emphasized that all the law could be summed up in two commandments: love the Lord your God with all your heart, and your neighbor as yourself. He also taught another version of the golden rule: don't do anything to others which you would find abhorrent if done to you.

According to Matthew 27:25 the Pharisees and Sadducees said to Pilate, "His blood be upon us and on our children." However, this did not mean a majority of the people or of the Pharisees supported the death of Jesus and accepted that responsibility. Nor does it mean that Jesus or God wanted anything done to the Jews for revenge. Jesus cried on the cross, "Forgive them!"

The passionate hatred some Christians display to the Jews illustrates how deep is the vengeance instinct and how great the desire to find scapegoats among minority peoples. One of the greatest injustices of all time has been the revenge of Christians against the Jews for presumably having killed Jesus.

Those identifying themselves as Christians have been the most anti-Jewish in the history of the world. Hitler, for instance, used the passion play of Oberammergau to whip up anti-Jewish feelings in Nazi Germany. In the name of Jesus there has been massive capital punishment.

### Christian Theology

When Christians think of the cross, they think of atonement. Jesus died for our sins. The idea is that sins have to be punished. We are all deserving of death. Jesus represented humanity on the cross and took the punishment we all deserve.

This theology comes in part from one of the servant songs of Isaiah. "Because of our sins he was wounded, beaten because of the evil we did. We are healed by the punishment he suffered, made whole by the blows he received" (Isaiah 53:5).

This, however, was only one of the servant songs. Jesus identified more clearly with Isaiah 61:1, "The Sovereign Lord has filled me with his spirit. He has chosen me and sent me to bring good news to the poor, to heal the broken-hearted, to announce release to captives."

These servant songs reveal that God does not act in a heavy-handed way. Rather, God gives strength and determination to accept suffering as a result of political action. Gandhi's nonviolent action and the suffering his supporters were prepared to endure illustrate the suffering servant role.

The Jewish people as a community have seen themselves in this role. The point of the servant song is not to glorify suffering. Rather, it shows how hard it is to work for justice, a justice which empowers the poor and weak in society.

## The Power of Evil

The power of evil was at work. *Diabolos*, the Greek word for devil, means "to throw between." The power of evil drives wedges between those who are close. Jesus had been tempted by the devil to accept the world's power. Jesus refused to be subverted. By accepting the *means* of the devil he would have lost his connectedness to humanity.

The cross symbolizes the rejection of evil means to gain power.

### Atonement and Forgiveness

Christian theology of atonement is like the "once for all" theology found in Judaism. There was a sense that any capital punishment teaching had to be carried out only once. That is one reason so few executions were recorded in the Bible. The Flood, for example, was a once-for-all-time response to pervasive rebellion against the ways of God.

Another understanding was that of transference of guilt. The atonement rituals transferred guilt to an animal.

The idea of a merciful God ready to forgive was there all along. The prophets made clear that the quality of one's heart was more important than sacrificial rituals.

If Jesus died once for all, taking on the guilt of the world, he died even for those who committed the most abhorrent crimes. Forgiveness means giving up the right to revenge or punish.

### Summary

Because Jews argued that Jesus be crucified, Christians have wrongly taken out their vengeful feelings on the Jews. Jesus' death involved a struggle with the forces of evil. His death illustrates that working for justice will likely involve suffering. It also means that forgiveness is available to anyone who is deserving of death.

### Questions for Reflection and Discussion

1. Rather than seek revenge on his tormentors,

Jesus prayed for their forgiveness. How can we go about turning over to God the fate of our oppressors?

2. Who today is suffering for the work he or she is doing for justice?

3. Reflect on the meaning of mercy and forgiveness.

# CHAPTER 9

# *What Is Justice?*

"Crime is a disease. Meet the cure."

These words appeared in an advertisement for the movie *Cobra*.

The ad shows what people expect in justice. Not a sensitive administration of law, but an overwhelming force seeking revenge. Through force of muscle and technology, the problem will be solved. People will get both protection (the strong arm of the law) and the "joy" of getting even with all who are hurting them.

Do we really want a government characterized by a "get-tough" mentality? What about the statement "Crime is a disease. Meet the cure"? The ad suggests that the cure is radical surgery—cutting out, or cutting down the bad people. The "war-on-crime" mentality carries an ironic twist: it supposes that a life-destroying revenge can be the means to a life-giving cure.

Many Christians support this image of government with a sentence taken out of context from Romans 13. Verse 4 is translated a variety of ways. Note the following:

For he is the minister of God to thee for good. But if thou do that which is evil, be afraid; for he beareth not the sword in vain: for he is the minister of God, a revenger to execute wrath upon him that doeth evil. (King James Version)

The policeman is sent by God to help you. But if you are doing something wrong, of course you should be afraid, for he will have you punished. He is sent by God for that very purpose.

(Living Bible)

The state is there to serve God for your benefit. If you break the law, however, you may well have fear: the bearing of the sword has its significance. The authorities are there to serve God: they carry out God's revenge by punishing wrongdoers.

(Jerusalem Bible)

Some even go so far as to use this verse in support of capital punishment.

Before making the leap from a 1,930-year-old letter to public policy today, let's be certain we know what Paul was talking about. It is not immediately evident whether he is talking about the state, the policeman, or something else.

Paul, the author of Romans, had trained as a Pharisee. All his life he had been committed to serving God. At one point in his life he considered Jesus to be a false teacher. He thought he could serve God by *persecuting* the followers of Jesus.

Then, on his way to Damascus, he had an experience in which his vision of Jesus changed. He continued to serve God zealously. But now he was interested in establishing a church in which Jews and Gentiles could be united under Christ.

In Romans 9–11 Paul develops a worldview that makes it possible for Jewish and Gentile Christians to respect one another within the church. Chapters 12–15 point out the ethical dimensions—how to live a good life in a hostile environment.

Near the end of chapter 12, Paul quotes two passages from the Hebrew Bible: "I will take revenge, I will pay back," says the Lord (Deuteronomy 32:35). "If your enemy is hungry, feed him; if he is thirsty, give him a drink; for by doing this, you will make him burn with shame" (Proverbs 25:21-22).

Paul uses these quotes to make three points: (1) don't seek vengeance; (2) live peacefully with everyone; (3) conquer evil with good. He then applies these to the relationship between the Roman Christians and the state, which opposed them.

Paul's arguments are both moral and practical. On the practical side, he argues that if people resort to evil means, they will get in trouble. Furthermore, by doing good, one can anticipate praise even from an evil state. Paul also argues that since power comes from God, God will hold people accountable for how they use that power. Therefore the Roman Christians ought not be too quick to "take the law into their own hands" or to launch a revolt against those who dominate society. The rulers are servants of God to do good. And if they do evil, they are responsible to *God.*

The point is that the Roman Christians are to pay their taxes and respect the government. Paul is concerned that their testimony not be colored by a rebellious attitude. The Christians are not to seek revenge against the state. He is realistic enough to know that if they rebel against the state and do things which are hurtful, the state will hold them accountable. "It is not for nothing that they bear the sword," says Paul.

Paul tells the Romans that those ruling society have real power to be feared. Paul is not suggesting that the Roman government *ought* to be punishing or taking vengeance. Rather, Paul is trying to prevent Christians from getting in trouble for the wrong reasons.

Paul spells out what this means more concretely in Galatians. After listing behaviors associated with evil, Paul lists the fruit of the Spirit: love, joy, peace, gentleness, etc. At the end of this list, he states, "Against such there can be no law." His aim was to instruct the Christian community so its behavior would rise above reproach.

The book of Revelation was written at a time when persecution was far more widespread. In its own symbolic way, it associates the government of its time with the power of evil. There is no hint that the Roman emperor is an agent of God.

None of the New Testament was written when Christians had real power within society. Jesus associated with the outcasts of society. The church of Peter and Paul was a tiny group, threatened by divisions within and enemies without. The churches of the book of Revelation feared for their lives. Chapter 13 represents the government as a beast with the powers of a totalitarian regime. Those wishing to use *Romans* 13 to legitimate the use of force by the state ought to temper their attitudes with this graphic imagery from *Revelation* 13.

Within Canada, the United States, and Western Europe are people with real power who look to the

Bible for an understanding of right and good. Certainly biblical principles of mercy, love, and goodness have wide application.

The dynamics are similar to the teachings of Jesus discussed above. When he wished to make an impact upon the lives of his hearers, he stressed the outcome of their actions. When talking of the response to injustice, he stressed love in response to hate.

Paul is doing the same. He is trying to influence the actions of Christians, not the Roman emperor. In the book of Acts, we find some of Paul's speeches to political authorities. He spoke the truth boldly and at times confronted the authorities with the injustices he had suffered.

*Revelation* offers encouragement to the persecuted—hope that the power of God is the power that matters in the end. Unlike the recipients of Paul's letter to the Romans, the Christians who received the *Revelation* would not have considered mounting a rebellion against the emperor.

### Summary

I started this chapter noting that "the strong arm of the law" is a popular ideal image of the state. This differs significantly from the image of the suffering servant working for justice. From Romans we get the message that the state, as it existed at the time of Paul, was strong on law and order and that it really was to be feared. Paul does not want the small Christian community of Rome to be destroyed in a political rebellion.

The Bible emphasizes throughout the need to uphold the interests of the poor and the weak. This is a more logical starting point than looking for ways to justify punishment.

In the preceding chapters, I have examined many of the most crucial and difficult texts pertaining to the death penalty.

We first noted that the strongest biblical statement favoring the death penalty is made in a context least likely to require it. The warning is pointed at whatever threatens a community the most.

The listing of "capital offenses" stands in contrast to community values and makes the point that all have sinned.

As we examined the death penalty teachings related to murder, we found an emphasis on preventing speedy revenge. The application of these teachings within the Jewish community practically ruled out the death penalty.

When the whole community deserved to die, God's anger was restrained and provided new opportunities for the people. This did not do away with the outcome of evil acts but provided an opportunity for God's creative action.

We raised the question, "Could Jesus really be associated with the death penalty?" Jesus' teachings suggest that believers should be aware of the results of their actions when they contemplate wrongdoing. In response to evil, Jesus suggests doing good. To the sinner he offers the hope of forgiveness and restoration.

The death of Jesus prompted revenge on the Jews. His death meant that working for justice could bring suffering to us. The atoning dimension means that forgiveness is available to everyone.

After exhaustive and exhausting study of the subject, I find no justification in Scripture for a current application of the death penalty or revenge killing. Though there may be pictures of such, Scripture does not appear to advocate it.

This does not mean the Scriptures aren't helpful in meeting the dilemmas facing society. On the contrary, the Bible contains a great deal of material concerning victims, offenders, and the life of communities. These stories show suffering and pain, but also hope.

## Questions for Reflection and Discussion

1. Reread the above summary of key points from chapters 1-9.

2. Identify points of agreement or questions that remain.

PART TWO

# Steps for Responding
# to Violent Crime

# CHAPTER 10

# *Get Out of the Rut*

A church organization recently asked me to draft a new statement on capital punishment for consideration at its annual meeting.

As I began to reflect on the assignment, I soon saw that most official statements on the death penalty argue either for or against it. Those arguing against it are often defensive and negative. Why not consider a positive statement? I thought.

The ideas started to flow. Out of the challenge came *A Call to Action on Abhorrent Crimes.* The people calling for the death penalty do so out of a sense of frustration over the most abhorrent crimes—rape and murder (especially of children), terrorism, and the killing of police officers. The real question is, "How can we deal with these crimes?" To only say, "We are against the death penalty," leaves people with a sense of frustration. There seems to be no last word against crime.

Those who speak out against capital punishment have not been effective in denouncing abhorrent crime. By not expressing strong feelings about violent crimes, we have left the impression that we are "soft" on crime. Whether or not we know the offender, we must communicate our shock and horror over those events which deeply disturb our community.

As I considered how to respond to violent crime, I concluded that the first thing is *to be present in a special way with victims*. In doing this, we show the love of a God who hears the cries of victims.

The offender, too, needs special care. When suspects are apprehended and convicted, they need to be surrounded by people prepared to listen to their deep feelings of guilt and hurt. *We need to listen to offenders* as they share the events of their lives which led to their criminal acts. The God of the Bible is a God who reaches out to both offenders and victims.

To denounce a crime does not mean writing off the criminal. If we wish to gain the insight needed to prevent future crime, we must learn to understand the circumstances that lead a person to commit criminal acts.

My relationship with both victims and offenders have shown me how complex the problem of crime is. People react differently to similar crimes. To get beyond the hurt, *we must find the truth.* Unfortunately, our courts spend more time proving blame than seeking truth. The Bible, however, emphasizes the liberating dimensions of truth.

Crime has severe consequences for both victims and offenders. They feel these results for years. As we move from the truth of what *happened,* we need to look at the truth of what *is happening* as a result. Sometimes the punishment people bring upon themselves is more severe than that handed out by the criminal justice system. To put things in perspective, we need a clear explanation of what has happened because of the crime.

With an awareness of the truth and its consequences, we can begin to *discern options* for victims, offenders, and the communities injured by crime. We need creative thinking because each crime is unique and involves unique people—creative because creation is life-generating.

Violent crime is like death. It limits choices and separates people. In the face of death, it is difficult to expand choices and bring people together, *but choices must be made*. With fresh options we must choose the ones most suited to the situation. But who should choose and how do we choose?

Finally, we must provide *long-term follow-up*. Victims and offenders are usually forgotten, ignored, or isolated. How many people visit the lifers in prison? How many remember their victims? God took an interest in a murderer named Moses 40 years after his crime. Many of the psalms reflect on victimization.

## Questions for Reflection and Discussion

1. Identify several positive responses to violent crime.

2. What course of action helps to get beyond the hurt?

3. How can the Christian community oppose capital punishment without appearing soft on crime?

# CHAPTER 11

# *Be Present with Victims*

Over ten years ago, my wife and I returned home to find that a burglar had been there. Our first emotion was fear. Was he still in the house? How did he get in? Was he angry? Had he carried a gun? What was missing? Would he come back?

We felt hurt and sadness as we realized that our few valuable possessions were stolen. Not only had they taken the stereo, but also a favorite record on the turntable and my wife's box of jewelry. Her friendship rings from the past were irreplaceable.

Our hurt turned to anger. It seemed so pointless since any items sold would yield only a fraction of the value they had to us.

For a year we examined the house every time we came home in the evening to see if a burglar had been there. Just as our anxiety level began to diminish, we experienced another break-in. The burglar took a cheap swag lamp and our son's quarter-size violin. Once again, we went through the emotions of fear, hurt, and anger.

Years after the two break-ins, we chose not to

buy a home bordering a woods. The trauma of our burglaries dictated a more secure location.

If the effects of a break-in are so severe, how much worse the effects of violent crime! I cannot imagine the devastation at the loss of one of my children. Whatever the crime, it is not right to leave victims alone. They need the support of their friends and neighbors, the help of the wider community, and the opportunity to voice their deepest pain in their church. I will illustrate these means of support from Scripture and then offer suggestions for action.

### The Support of Friends and Neighbors

"Two are better off than one. . . . If one of them falls down, the other can help him up" (Ecclesiastes 4:9-10). "Weep with those who weep" (Romans 12:15).

Victims of violent crime feel powerless, afraid, and isolated. They feel rejected by God and betrayed by humanity. It becomes hard for them to trust anyone.

Nothing can compare to a friend who cares when one is hurting. Someone whose emotions are stable can act as an anchor for one who is upset. One whose emotions can stretch to weep with the wailing can enter into the lonely space of sorrow.

There are many practical things we can do for victims of abhorrent crimes. Some want protection. Some need shelter, others child care.

In 1985 the son of friends died in the Air India disaster. Members of the community surrounded our friends. Some mourned with them. Others simply listened to their thoughts and recollections of their son. A group of us watched the television reports together. Some friends helped attend to practical concerns, such as looking after meals. Others offered strength and comfort by their steady presence. This illustrates that friends can support victims in many different ways.

On the other hand, the public sometimes seems out to "crush" the offender. Punishment rather than restoration and healing seems to be the primary concern. Offenders, of course, influence the public reaction by their attitudes and words. When victims hear that the offenders are sorry for their crime, hatred can turn to pity and caring. When offenders say they have no regrets and would do it again, their victims find it hard to think in constructive terms. They need reassurance that such people can never again savagely harm people.

### Laments in the Churches

Words cannot express the deep pain and anguish of many victims. Not only have they suffered pain and loss, they feel the bereavement is unnecessary and unjust. Many feel abandoned and rejected by God. Often victims transfer the guilt to themselves.

All victims have feelings of revenge. Many fantasize in detail how they might torture the offenders. One woman who lost a child to a killer, enrolled in a university, got a degree in criminology, and took a job in the prison where the offender was held. She took a gun into her office and asked to see the prisoner. At the last moment, she decided not to kill him. The process of acting out her fantasy of revenge took six years.

When a victim is feeling guilty, hurt, and vengeful, sermons about the goodness of God and the joy of salvation do not fit well with their experience. Nor do they fit the biblical understanding of prayer. No fewer than 20 out of 150 psalms are victims' laments. Often when these are read in churches, the strongest expressions of anger, fear, and revenge are omitted. Consider the following lament.

> LORD, you are a God who punishes;
> reveal your anger!
> You are the judge of all men;
> rise and give the proud what they deserve!
>
> How much longer will the wicked be glad?
> How much longer, LORD?
> How much longer will criminals be proud
> and boast about their crimes?
>
> They crush your people, LORD;
> they oppress those who belong to you.
> They kill widows and orphans,
> and murder the strangers who live in our land.
>
> They say, "The LORD does not see us;
> the God of Israel does not notice."
> My people, how can you be such stupid fools?
> When will you ever learn?          (Psalm 94:1-8)

In this psalm, God is called upon to take revenge. As Walter Brueggemann points out, it is left up to God to decide how and when to do this.

God does not fall apart when people get angry. The Lord does not need protection from the hurtful, angry, guilty, and vengeful feelings of victims. It may be that God can only begin working with their situation when they lay out their grief in prayer and lament. In any case, it can be helpful to victims to have a place in which to pour out their hearts before God and the faith community.

So what can the church do for victims? It can provide this place for victims to express their fear, anger, and grief. Perhaps we need special services for this. Lay and clergy counselors trained in handling grief can help with this process.

Some victims may wish to use the psalms in the Bible. Others will want to write their own laments.

## Questions for Reflection and Discussion

1. What attitude should we have toward violent crime? Should we seek punishment or restoration?

2. We noted a biblical practice for victims to deal with their anger. What is it?

3. How can a community truly be present with victims?

4. Why is the Christian community uncomfortable with psalms of lament and revenge? What ought our attitude be?

CHAPTER 12

# Denounce the Action

Nothing stirs emotions like violent crime. That is why terrorists use violence to make a statement. They want the world to notice them. That is also why the community needs to express feelings publicly. Leaders can denounce violent actions even if the perpetrators are unknown.

The prophets effectively denounced actions they found morally and legally unacceptable. The actions they exposed and denounced were the ones described in chapter 3 as capital offenses. Here are some examples of how they denounced crime:

> You are doomed! You buy more houses and fields
>     to add to those you already have.
> Soon there will be no place for anyone else
>     to live,
>     and you alone will live in the land.    (Isaiah 5:8)

> You are doomed! You make unjust laws
>     that oppress my people.
> That is how you keep the poor from
>     having their rights and from getting justice.
>                                         (Isaiah 10:1-2)

We notice from these brief excerpts that the prophets aimed their denunciation at behaviors which destroy communities. They not only pointed to the acts of common criminals, but also to the acts of leaders who were acting immorally.

The prophets used symbols the people easily understood. At times the denunciation ridiculed. For example, people who called idols "father" implied that the idols had conceived them.

When Jesus denounced the selling of sacrifices for profit in the temple, he not only quoted Jeremiah 7:11 ("You have made the temple into a robbers' den"), he turned over the tables.

Churches and society have not been effective in denouncing abhorrent actions. Maybe like the ancients, we should wear torn clothing to show remorse over an event. We fly flags at half-staff when an important person dies, but we seldom do it after an abhorrent crime.

Sometimes persons who are angry at political leaders for policies which are morally wrong burn them in effigy. This is a symbolic action of denunciation, but it also shows a vengeful, violent spirit. We need prayers of denunciation, songs of denunciation, dramas of denunciation, and pictures of denunciation. They would express the damage done by acts of violence without expressing vengeance.

We need to depict the fear of walking the streets, the worry of parents in a community that has lost a child, the emptiness of meaning when a leader has been killed.

Denunciation shows that the evil is not overcoming the community. It reinforces positive values in the population and supports the victims by affirming their grief.

Could we not find symbols to lead the community both to denounce the action and show a resolve not to let abhorrent crime control everyone? When fear of crime results in so much defensive action that our lifestyle becomes oppressive, the criminal has won. He or she is in control.

Reflect on the imagery in Psalm 10. It denounces evil, yet calls the oppressed to hope. At present, the only way society regularly denounces criminal acts is to send the criminal to prison for a long time. But this depends upon a conviction. Most crimes are not solved.

Prison brutalizes the offender unnecessarily because it does not restore the person to wholeness of life in the community.

## Questions for Reflection and Discussion

1. List ways you might denounce violent crime in your community.

2. What purpose would it serve?

3. How should we treat an offender who is caught?

# CHAPTER 13

# *See Prisoners as Humans*

At one point I thought of prisoners as prisoners: similar, nameless bodies. When I started visiting prisoners, I was shocked to realize they were real people. They differed from one another as any group of people from the street might differ from one another.

For every individual caught and convicted of a crime, there are *two* persons. One is a monster, the other is a human being. The monster is the public image of a demonic character with no history. It just appears as a fearsome beast. Anyone is a potential victim of the monster. The only way for society to protect itself from the monster is to put the monster in a cage.

The other criminal is a person. She or he may have been a victim of child abuse or have learning disabilities. She or he may have come from a poor, single-parent family or may have grown up on the street. It may be that within this person's culture it is a mark of distinction to do time in prison.

If the person has killed another person, he or

she may have been provoked by a perceived injustice. The victim may have been unfaithful in marriage or behind in payments on a gambling or drug debt. He or she may have told a lie for unfair advantage or turned somebody in.

If the offender has robbed a bank or broken into a home, it may well have been to support a drug habit. It could also have resulted from years of trying to get a job or of receiving a wage that made it impossible to live well.

Often offenders and the communities that produced them are victims who have never experienced justice. No one has denounced the evil done to them. No one has lamented with them. They are forgotten by the world.

I do not mean to justify criminal activity but to point to the many unfortunate factors that may have contributed to it. The more society gives the criminal a monster role, the better the chance that person will accept this role. The media and the criminal justice system have excellent monster-making capabilities. When people cry out for the death penalty, they are asking that the monsters be killed. If they get to know the *people*, they tend to change their position on capital punishment.

The message of the Bible is that God loves each person even though all have sinned. We should thus be reluctant to judge another person. Our first action when facing an evildoer is to listen.

In time, it is important to hold offenders accountable. They need to know the damage they have done. They need to know the deep hurt and suffering they have caused. But they will be more open if they feel they, too, have been heard.

A friend of mine worked many years as prison chaplain. Throughout his career, his wife and young children were involved in his ministry. They visited prisoners and took them into their homes. When my friend's house was robbed by a burglar, his daughters suffered severe emotional trauma. They couldn't sleep. Or when they slept, they had nightmares. They were afraid to leave the house, and they feared entering the house when they returned.

When the story of their reaction was told in prison, several break-in artists said they had never considered the human side of their action. They began to feel extreme remorse over the emotional suffering they may have caused some little children.

A recent issue of *Psychology Today* says that the suicide rate in short-term holding centers is ten times that of the general population. Many young men and women take their own lives shortly after being caught because they are overcome with feelings of guilt and despair.

If this system is harsh enough with them, these feelings can turn to self-pity and hatred. Offenders start to feel like victims, especially during a long prison term. Their needs are similar to victims. Through the process, they begin to forget about their victims and the hurt they have caused.

Many persons in the Bible committed crimes. As offenders with whom God was present, they were people, not monsters. Adam and Eve were the first. Cain's life continued after being a murderer. He even had the blessing of children and grandchildren.

The Bible also contains the stories of nameless

"monsters" who were destroyed—victims of the Flood, members of Pharaoh's army, and the peoples of Canaan destroyed by the invading Hebrews.

As one reflects on the stories of the Bible, one thing becomes clear. The *actions* of the "monsters" need to be denounced, but the *people* need to be cared for. God loves every person.

When the prophets thought about the end of history, they envisioned people from "every tribe and nation" worshiping God together. They saw in their vision everyone being changed from a monster to a person.

When Jesus ministered to outcasts—the publicans, sinners, and prostitutes—he made people out of monsters. This was his mission.

## Questions for Reflection and Discussion

1. What turns criminals into monsters? How can we prevent this from happening?

2. What turns monsters into people? How can we be a part of this?

# CHAPTER 14

# *Search Out the Truth*

We face two problems when we try to find out what really happened in an abhorrent crime. The first is that people lie a lot. The second is that the courts are not as concerned to establish truth as to establish blame.

In a court setting, the accused is obviously threatened. He or she can flee by not telling the truth or can fight by making accusations. If the threat is strong enough and emotions are high, accusations may be stretched or even invented.

Similarly the victim is threatened: by reprisals from the offender if immediately released. And by the frustration of nothing being done about the crime if the offender is found not guilty.

Defense lawyers have as their goal the release of their clients. If they can use delays and fine points of the law to help their clients get off a charge, they will do it. These technicalities have nothing to do with the truth of what happened.

It is a myth of the North American legal system that people are considered innocent until proven guilty. It is technically true that people cannot be sentenced until proven guilty. Police and prosecutors, however, do not treat suspects as though they were innocent. They often assume guilt. Their challenge is to prove it to a judge or jury.

A defense lawyer who knows a client is guilty acts not on this truth, but rather to protect the client. A guilty client is advised to plead "not guilty." This means, "I don't think you can prove that I did it." It does *not* mean, "I hereby declare that I did not commit the offense for which I am charged."

This adversary system has grown from the principle that people ought to be protected from favoritism and false accusation. This protection can be subverted into a legalism standing in the way of solving problems. Many have a vested interest in preserving the system. Further, since the community sees the criminal justice system as responsible for protection, order, and security, few are willing to challenge it.

The Bible gives considerable priority to searching out and admitting the truth. Adam and Eve were confronted when they ate the fruit. Cain was held accountable for killing Abel. Lots were cast to discover that Aachan had stolen goods from Jericho. The prophets were preoccupied with telling the truth. Jesus bitterly denounced hypocrisy—a form of lying. He taught the importance of confrontation to establish truth in a dispute.

Let us agree on the problem: people *do* lie to protect themselves or to hurt others. The greater the threat or the higher the stakes, the greater the temptation to lie. Let us also agree that seeking the truth is an honorable activity.

*Truth for Victims*

A young woman is raped and knifed to death. The offender pleads not guilty. With the help of a good lawyer, he escapes conviction. He is released into the community. The parents of the young woman feel hurt and afraid. They are angry partly because nothing was done and partly because the truth did not come out.

When Elizabeth Morris lost a son to a drunk driver, she built up a hatred for the man who killed him. That hatred ebbed when the offender finally admitted he had killed her son. The truth liberated Elizabeth from negative feelings consuming her.

Later the offender gave a speech to high school students. He admitted publicly what he had done and showed remorse for his actions. This continued the healing process. Eventually, Elizabeth forgave him and started to care for him. Without his telling the truth, this could not have happened.

Gerry Ruygrok lost his daughter in a halfway house murder. For him, it was important to find the truth about the system and the process that contributed to the murder. Though bereaved, he participated in a coroner's inquest and personally questioned people from the prison and parole systems.

At the end of the inquest, he was universally praised for the spirit with which he tried not to establish blame, but to *seek the truth*. The inquest uncovered a list of recommendations for change—recommendations the Solicitor General of Canada is taking seriously.

Many unanswered questions surround murders, rapes, and acts of terrorism. Only the offender can answer many of them. To understand what happened and why it happened does not reverse the clock, but it does help to set minds at ease.

In offenses against children, the truth becomes even more important. One victim of incest told me her mother's unwillingness to believe her story was as hard to accept as the incest itself. She began to question her own sanity. It was harder than ever to sort out the truth. The same is true when an offender is found "not guilty." To a child, this means no one believes the offense happened.

For victims who fear the system, there is no avenue for reporting crime. These victims suffer "in the closet." With domestic violence or sexual abuse, thousands suffer long without anyone knowing. This "invisible" suffering is one of the greatest tragedies of suppressing truth.

The psychiatric profession and observers of the criminal justice system acknowledge that victims are thrice victimized. First by the crime. Second by the criminal justice system. Third by themselves.

They often blame themselves. They feel guilty for having been victims. Sometimes they feel dirty. Understanding the long and tangled roots leading to a crime helps victims release themselves from the endless circles of grief and guilt.

If we really want to restore victims to mental health, we must find better ways to seek the truth.

### Truth for Offenders

Offenders have the most to fear from an exposure of the truth. Our system shields them from the full truth of what they have done by keeping them away from victims.

They do suffer guilt, but it is often diffused. Not knowing all the results of their actions, it is easy for them to rationalize what they have done.

As offenders start to do time in prison, they themselves become victims. Guards strip-search them and make fun of them in the process. They may become victims of rape by fellow prisoners. Extortion and "head games" round out the prison experience.

People who are rewarded for lying and punished for truthtelling (as is the case when people turn themselves in) find it difficult to learn to search for and speak the truth. A subculture based on lying and deceit is hard to turn around.

Jeremiah knew this:

> They are all unfaithful, a mob of traitors.
> They are always ready to tell lies;
>     dishonesty instead of truth rules the land.
>                                  (Jeremiah 9:2-3)

To break the cycle of falsehood, prisoners need to experience the joy and pain of letting truth emerge. They need to be treated with good faith. They need a nonthreatening context in which they can explore the truth of what they have done and how they have done it. They need to hear the pain, hurt, and rage of victims.

Why? Only when they have been held fully accountable for their actions can they move ahead responsibly. Only when they have confessed what they have done, can they get beyond it.

## Truth for the Community
Many communities go on with unanswered ques-

tions about tragic events. The Air India disaster of 1985 is one such case. The final report said it was the result of a bomb, but there has not yet been a trial at which some of the story might be told.

There is no simple formula for getting at the truth. Immunity, however, helps. The U.S. Senate committee investigating the Irangate affair, for example, granted immunity to several key witnesses. Immunity creates a nonthreatening atmosphere for the people involved. Usually it is used only to release information to convict others who do not get the benefit of immunity.

When we fix blame and put an offender in prison, we deal only with the most obvious part of the crime. The hard part is to deal with the roots—the truth of the suffering experienced by both victims and offenders.

It is hard to get at the truth. People lie. The system does not encourage the exposure of truth. And the truth is usually deep and complex. If we want the kind of justice which leaves everyone satisfied, we have no choice but to search vigorously for the truth. That involves creating contexts and institutions which help the truth to emerge.

## Questions for Reflection and Discussion

1. How does the present criminal justice system subvert the truth?

2. How can we encourage criminals to tell the truth?

3. What discourages offenders from telling the truth?

# CHAPTER 15

# *Show Consequences and Give Choices*

A *consequence* is the suffering that follows naturally from wrongdoing. *Punishment* is the suffering imposed on the person who has done wrong. Punishment is usually decided by a judge or jury. It comes from the outside.

Some consequences are personal. For instance, a child playing with fire may get his or her fingers burned. Other consequences are relational. Because Moses had killed an Egyptian, he had to leave Egypt and live in the desert for 40 years. No one sentenced him to such a term. He knew that both Hebrews and Egyptians were so angry with him he would lose his life if he stayed. Because David murdered Uriah, he had considerable dissension within his family.

Often the consequences of a crime are harder to accept than arbitrary punishment. That is why it is important to tell the full story of a crime. Some judges feel they need to give harsh sentences to deter people from abhorrent crime. A more effective deterrent may be to require offenders to tell the complete truth.

I once knew a young man who hit his father on the head with a two-by-four. The father became paralyzed from the neck down. Before going to prison, the son helped to look after his father. Every day, as he fed his father and helped him in and out of bed, he was reminded of the event. Daily he suffered guilt and remorse. The inner pain was terrible.

I proposed a sentence to the judge which would have included care of the father. But the judge sentenced the young man to prison to signal to the community that this was a serious crime.

Sometimes we think that exposing wrongdoing is not enough. We have to have *punishment*. But for public figures, the pain of exposure can be severe. The negative consequences we bring upon ourselves are often harder to bear than the arbitrary punishment others might impose.

Dealing with abhorrent crime must therefore include naming the consequences for the offender, the victim, and the community. This endeavor is similar to that of seeking the truth. In the previous chapter, I tried to show the importance of under standing the circumstances, emotions, and events that contributed to a criminal act. In this chapter, I have argued that the same search for truth ought to be brought to bear on the present (the after-crime present) and the future.

### Acknowledge the Consequences

Klaus Barbie, a Nazi war criminal, was brought to

trial a few years ago. Shortly after the trial began, he refused to come to the courtroom. The victims found this most disappointing because they felt the need to tell their stories directly to him.

It is important for victims that offenders say what has happened to them as a result of the criminal act. It is also important for victims and the community to be aware of the offenders' feelings of guilt. They need to tell of the panic they felt when they were discovered and the fear that engulfed them as they tried to escape detection. The offender needs to feel the grief of the victim.

Sometimes this happens through a direct meeting. Or someone could interview the parents of a murder victim on videotape. They could talk about their experiences, their hopes for the child, and what the child meant to them. The murderer could then view the video and respond.

Many offenders have such deep guilt they find it hard to put it in words. Prison culture demands that they appear strong. To survive they have to pretend and deceive. To express real feelings makes them appear weak and open to attack.

Not acknowledging a terrible crime causes bitterness in victims. This happened to Ukranians as a community when Stalin and Soviet historians refused to admit that millions of their people were killed in the 1930s.

A realization of the consequences of crime can be extremely painful—more painful than prison. The result, however, can bring healing. For the victim, the offender's acknowledgment can open the door for forgiveness and inner healing.

## Give Options

After an abhorrent crime, victims and offenders go on living. Many live in a kind of hell. Some victims live in fear and distrust for the rest of their lives. Hatred and vengeful feelings can dominate their lives. For offenders, life imprisonment brings hopelessness and despair.

Those are not the only options. If they tell the truth and admit the consequences of the crime, the way is open for life-giving options—options not easy, but better than a living death.

If communities are a part of the process of acknowledging consequences, it is no longer important to punish offenders. The pain and suffering is already present and apparent to everyone. It is not necessary to add to this pain. It is important, however, to offer protection to the community. The security of victims and communities *is* important—especially since making choices and realizing change may take time.

One must be clear on a vision for the future. What exactly do victims and offenders and communities wish to accomplish through the options?

Each option has a price tag. The average annual cost of keeping a person in prison may be $50,000. Court costs can be enormous. Suppose there were five cases of serious domestic violence in one community. Four men and one woman were caught and sent to prison for three years. If a way could be found to transfer the $250,000 per year into the community for services to families in trouble, the community might achieve better results.

The offending parties could live in separate apartments and be ordered to stay in them unless they went to work or to a treatment program. They could see their families occasionally under supervision. If counselors could help them establish trusting, nonabusing relationships, they might be reunited with their families after a time. If not, they could work out the details of a separation.

If the primary goal is protection, special villages may need to be established for those who cannot live in their communities of origin. Life might be normal within these villages, except that the residents would not be allowed to leave for a time.

The prophets say Israel was deported to Babylon because the Israelites forgot God. Many of the offenses associated with death in chapter 3 were religious. Had these death penalty teachings been applied literally, the people would have been reduced to nothing. Instead they were only deported.

One of the options for them was to plan an escape. Jeremiah suggested a different option: to build houses in Babylon and settle down. That is what they did. This was not easy. Psalm 137 talks of weeping by the rivers of Babylon. Some of the most insightful material in the Bible came out of the Babylonian Exile.

Intense pain and disruption can cause creativity and life—or vengeful hatred—to develop. We *do* have choices to make. The more creative we are at developing options, the better the chance of making wise decisions.

## Questions for Reflection and Discussion

1. What actions help offenders deal with their hurts in ways that bring healing?

2. What can be done to bring healing to victims?

# CHAPTER 16

# *Make Choices*

When a murder was committed among aboriginal peoples of North America, the elders would gather with the families of the offender and the victim. They would consider the crime and its effects and arrange a solution that fit the situation. Frequently, the murderer would join the family of the deceased to do the work of the victim.

Not every society has such flexibility. In Canada, judges have no choice in first-degree murder. The law requires them to give a life sentence with no possibility of parole for 25 years.

As we noted earlier, God's treatment of us is not dictated by that kind of legalism. When the whole community deserved death, Moses persuaded God not to destroy the people (Genesis 32:7-14).

But who should make the decision about which options to take? At present, it is up to judges to choose among limited options.

The idea of having judges pronounce sentence is based on the need for an independent opinion to hand down a sentence that fits. The image of a scales is common: punishment must roughly equal the crime.

But what if we conclude that punishment is not the right response to crime? We must look for an intervention to fit the context.

Judges should be part of the process. They play a mediating role. They also have the benefit of much experience and knowledge of the law. But their strength is also a weakness. Experience and knowledge of the law can produce a certain blindness. They may not see some possible new options.

Victims ought to be part of the process, too. They are most affected by the crime. Their pain has to be addressed. They suffer many consequences and have special needs. They bring the harsh realities of the situation to the process, which must be grounded in reality. Their strength may also become a weakness. The immediate pain of the victim may blur the longer view.

Offenders ought to be part of the process. Any option will affect them greatly. If their freedom is to be limited or if they are to be part of a treatment program, their voluntary participation in the decision will help produce positive results. Offenders wish for freedom more than anything. They are inclined to say and do "the right things" at the time of a decision to escape consequences they might not like.

Members of the communities of the victim and the offender ought to be included. Offenders are eventually released to a community. How the offender copes depends largely on what happens in the community.

Similarly the community of the victim is affected

by the crime and will want safeguards and protection. Community members can make all the difference in whether an alternate sentence will work. They can hold offenders accountable for their actions.

The police, probation officers, and parole officers ought to be a part of the sentencing process. They are the ones who must supervise the offender and hold him or her accountable to the plan decided upon. If they are aware of the variations in the process and the special concerns of the victim and the offender, they will more likely deal wisely with the situation.

If the plan includes loss of freedom, members of the restrictive community ought to be part of the process. After all, they must live with the offender day after day. The general principle is that those most affected by the aftermath of a crime ought to be a part of the process of dealing with it.

At present the criminal justice system cannot handle such a process. It is not structured for it. It may be up to local churches to assemble groups to develop options and make recommendations to the judge. Some judges may be willing to be a part of such an undertaking.

We have already pointed out that if the consequences of the crime are taken into account, punishment may not be needed. However, the community must be protected. The basic problems must be addressed so the crime is not likely to be repeated. And the offender must have a chance to do something to relieve the victim's hurt.

It takes energy and insight to work through a process which will be constructive to all concerned. In an era of microwave ovens and instant everything, it taxes our patience to deal with the shock of abhorrent crime. Not to take that time, however, may well leave vengeful feelings to fester and poison the future in some unexpected way.

As we develop ways to respond to abhorrent crimes, we must include those most affected by the criminal act: victims, offenders, and the communities in which they live. Judges, police, and the people who supervise the decision also have a role to play. They must allow time for the process on the one hand. On the other, people must know as soon as possible where they stand.

To make good decisions about options is only the beginning. There must be long-term follow-up to those most directly affected by a serious crime.

### Questions for Reflection and Discussion

1. Who needs to be involved in finding reconciliation for offenders and victims?

2. How can communities be protected from more violent crimes?

# CHAPTER 17

# *Take a Long-Term Interest*

Victims after a crime and offenders after conviction feel uprooted. Helpless. Barely able to survive. But the force of life is powerful. People do recover from harsh tragedies, although not everyone recovers fully.

It takes a long time for uprooted people to thrive again. Throughout that period, they may appear weak and vulnerable. Victims may need support for a decade or longer.

Last year our tomato plants got some frost late in spring. They looked so dreadful we almost pulled them out. They looked pitiful for a long time, but most of them finally survived. They never became healthy or as productive as they might have without the frost, but they still produced good tomatoes. But some of those plants didn't survive the frost. They never produced fruit.

The stress of abhorrent crime is too much for some people. Victims and offenders often feel that hope is gone. When the grief is unending, they may commit suicide. Offenders who start to think about a long prison sentence sometimes lose their will to live.

Society forgets those imprisoned for life. It is not right that they do not have some options to live life more fully. New life options *can* come out of painful events. The Christian message is that no one is beyond hope.

In ancient Israel, the people marked every seventh year to pay attention to those who had suffered severe misfortune. Every 50th year was devoted to meeting their needs. Debts were to be forgiven. Slaves were to be set free, and land was to return to its original owner.

The connection with crime may not be immediately apparent. People become poor through murder, extortion, and theft. In Bible times widows and orphans were the poorest in society.

When Jesus came preaching release to the captives and sight to the blind, he was talking about an era of Jubilee. In this time, hurting people would receive special attention.

Every now and then we ought to take stock of what has happened to victims in society. Some bereaved people remarry and successfully rebuild a future. Some, however, lead quiet, unnoticed lives of poverty and hurt. We need something to jolt us to attend to the needs around us.

If the year of Jubilee was a special time for *victims* in biblical Israel, the death of a priest was a special time for *offenders*. Those guilty of manslaughter had to stay in a city of refuge. It was like prison. They could leave if they wanted, but their lives would be in danger. When the priest died, however, they would be pardoned.

Such amnesties have been used for illegal aliens and persons who leave the country to avoid military training. They have allowed people living in fear to come forward and claim full citizenship.

We may need general amnesties for offenders from time to time. With careful planning, the emptying of our prisons could be a joyous event. It could symbolize for all of us release from the memories and feelings which hold us captive.

Long-term links need to be developed between victims and offenders. These relationships and how they are developed vary. Former sheriff Doug Call found that if victims receive support from the beginning, they usually want to meet the offender. The offenders find the meeting difficult. After the meeting the victims often feel like a burden has been lifted from their shoulders.

Sometimes it is enough for *similar* groups to meet each other. In Rochester, England, groups of bank robbers meet groups of bank tellers to explore the human dynamics of bank robberies. In Kitchener, Ontario, a self-help group of rape victims asked to meet with a similar group of rapists. The rapists were not the same people who had actually raped the victims.

One of the victims tried to show some feeling for the rapist. "I am beginning to understand you a little," she said, "but the one who raped me—he was an *animal*." All was quiet. The rapist then replied, "*I* was an animal."

Different people work on different timetables. Some victims of sexual abuse as children still have not fully faced their pain 25 years later.

Self-help groups for victims and offenders are

springing up everywhere. Victims of violence can help and support one another. Men who batter their wives can cut through the excuses and the denial of one another. People with similar experiences can help one another in a unique way because they understand each other.

Those in the community who have not had the same experience must find ways to help and to understand. Community members must learn to listen carefully to both victims and offenders. Churches have a special role to play since they can serve both the victim and the offender.

Storytelling can play helpful for all concerned. Stories free victims to share their pain and receive help and support. Once the pain is in the open, they can find release from their guilt.

It is with some hesitation that I mention the next point: forgiveness. Hesitation because the place of forgiveness is a sacred space. It cannot be entered into lightly. Sometimes pressure has been put on victims to forgive too soon. Pressure has also been put on victims not to forgive.

To go too quickly from mourning to dancing may be false healing. Never to allow for the dancing to come is to drown in despair.

### Summary

We have now looked at those elements which must be present to deal creatively with the aftermath of abhorrent crime. In some cases, people may want to change the ways they have dealt with crime, following the principles we have noted. Others may wish to start a victim support group or set up a context for truth-telling.

We may not be able to satisfy everyone. That should not stop us from trying to improve our ways of dealing constructively with crime.

Change often leads to other changes. To express the consequences of a crime, one may have to search for the roots of truth. Taking a long-term interest in victims and offenders will highlight the need to be present with victims right after a crime. So much is possible when there is a will to begin.

## Questions for Reflection and Discussion

1. Identify the Christian message for both victims and offenders.

2. What is the connection between poverty and crime?

3. Consider how you might help build long-term links between victims and offenders.

# CHAPTER 18

# *So What?*

Cliff and Wilma Derksen were Bible school colleagues of mine. I had lost touch with them for over 15 years.

Suddenly I became aware that they were the parents of Candace, a girl lost in Winnipeg. When her body was found, I mourned inwardly, for she was the same age as my oldest child.

In an article in *Mennonite Reporter* (May 11, 1987, p. 5), Wilma described her feelings about justice.

> Soon after the funeral, when I was still raw with grief, a friend came over. The tea was good, the room warm and quiet. She said, "Wilma, I know you have forgiven. I sense no vengeance. Knowing that, if you could let yourself go, what would satisfy justice for you? Would it be execution?"
>
> Till that point, I had never allowed myself the question. But I felt safe with her. Her question was a fair one, so I decided to explore my inner feelings.
>
> My first reaction was no, it wouldn't be enough. If the offender were executed, he would be dying

for something he had done and deserved. Candace died in the prime of her youth for no fault of her own. I groped for some kind of equity.

I was shocked when my answer was, "Ten child murderers would have to die . . . and I would have to pull the trigger." In my mind's eye, I saw 10 hooded figures lined up against a brick wall, and I pulled the trigger 10 times. The feeling was delicious.

The camera of my imagination continued to roll, and I saw the 10 hooded figures fall. I saw the blood and desecration. I saw the hoods fall loose and their faces vulnerable in death. I looked up and saw the mothers mourning the losses of their sons. And being so close to my own grief, I could identify fully and felt their losses as keenly as I felt my own. Even worse, I saw that one of the 10 had left no one to mourn his death. He had never had any love, and I had just snuffed out his last opportunity.

Coming back to reality, I was devastated. Christ showed how to flesh out the skeleton of justice with love and forgiveness. He showed that using our pain to build hope can bring complete healing. He knew more emptiness would follow if we seek to fill our loss with vengeance. He shows a better way to put value and meaning into our suffering.

Believing this, Cliff and I desperately tried to plant our little seeds of hope in our tragedy. We started a fund for a swimming pool at Camp Arnes. We helped start a Child Find organization in Winnipeg and shared our story openly as a test to see if this would fill the emptiness of our loss.

Nothing can replace Candace. But when I compare the delicious feeling of pulling the trigger to that wonderful, deep joy of seeing the swimming pool completed, finding a child, and knowing our story has helped others, there is no comparison.

The fantasy and reality of Wilma Derksen symbolize two courses of action. The first is the way of vengeance in which we use the death penalty for revenge. The second is the way of hope in which we make something new out of death and pain.

People feel powerless in the face of violent, abhorrent crime. This powerlessness turns to cynicism when the criminal justice system cannot offer total security against crime. We say the system doesn't work because the punishments are not harsh enough. According to this line of thought, it is reasonable to use the death penalty liberally.

The many decisions we make shape the character of our country. Some decisions are small and hardly make a dent in the scheme of things. Some are significant and can have long-term effects.

A decision about the death penalty is one of the latter. What does it do to our character to execute people? What does it do for us to deal creatively with abhorrent crime?

If we were to deal creatively with a few abhorrent crimes, what would that do for our society? Would it not offer hope for the smaller problems we face?

Our character also influences our decisions. If revenge is the way to deal with murder, is not revenge the way to deal with any other wrong? Maybe the death penalty is popular because most people in society deal with their problems in a vengeful kind of way. When we watch television, we constantly see revenge in action. Does television drama *reflect* who we are, or does it *shape* us?

The good thing about the death penalty debate is that it pushes us to make a decision. It forces us to be deliberate about our character, to take ownership in what we are about to become. We cannot decide by inaction.

What is the role of the church in the death penalty debate? Does the church have a role in shaping the character of a nation? Or do we wash our hands and let the state punish as it will?

Jesus and the prophets exposed evil by asking questions and telling stories. They did not hesitate to confront political authorities with the truth.

I have tried to show that some surprising insights emerge when one studies the Bible thoroughly. People like Wilma Derksen show what amazing things are possible if one begins to live a life of faith in forgiveness.

*Summary*

In this book we have reflected on the realities of crime and punishment from a biblical viewpoint. We began with the teaching of the Bible on the death penalty. My conclusion is that when we read the Bible in light of its language and culture of origin, it is not possible to sustain an argument for the death penalty on the basis of Scripture.

Thy word is a lamp unto my feet, and a light unto my path (Psalm 119:105, KJV).

## Questions for Reflection and Discussion

1. Do you agree that Scripture does not support the death penalty? Why or why not?

2. How might you become involved in the death penalty debate of your country?

3. Do you agree that our decision about the death penalty shapes what kind of society we are?

# References for Further Study

Boecker, Hans J., *Law and the Administration of Justice in the Old Testament and Ancient Near East*. Minneapolis: Augsburg Publishing House, 1978.

Daube, David, *Studies in Biblical Law*. New York: KTAV, 1969.

Dorff, Elliot N., "The Interaction of Jewish Law with Morality," *Judaism,* 26-4, Fall 1977.

Patrick, Dale, *Old Testament Law*. Atlanta: John Knox, 1985.

Swartley, Willard, ed., *The Bible and Law*. Elkhart Institute of Mennonite Studies, 1984.

Zehr, Howard, *Changing Lenses*. Scottdale, Pa.: Herald Press, 1990.

# *The Author*

Vernon W. Redekop works for the Church Council on Justice and Corrections in Ottawa. Ten denominations support the council, which provides leadership on issues of criminal justice.

He coordinates communications on a staff which shares leadership. His tasks include writing and editing publications, educational resources, and briefs to the government on criminal justice issues.

Before this he served as pastor in northern Manitoba, as administrator of the Montreal House of Friendship, as principal of Gouldtown Elementary School, and as a volunteer with Mennonite Brethren Missions and Services in Phoenix, Arizona.

He studied at the University of Saskatchewan (B. A. in philosophy, 1971; teacher's certificate, 1974) and at Mennonite Brethren Biblical Seminary in Fresno, California (M.A. in biblical studies, 1982).

Vernon and his wife, Gloria, are the parents of Quinn, Natasha, and Lisa. They live in Glouchester, Ontario, and are active in the Ottawa Mennonite Church.

# PEACE AND JUSTICE SERIES

*Edited by J. Allen Brubaker and Elizabeth Showalter*

This series of books sets forth briefly and simply some important emphases of the Bible regarding war and peace and how to deal with conflict and injustice. The authors write from within the Anabaptist tradition. This includes viewing the Scriptures as a whole as the believing community discerns God's Word through the guidance of the Spirit.

Some of the titles reflect biblical, theological, or historical content. Other titles in the series show how these principles and insights are practical in daily life.

1. *The Way God Fights* by Lois Barrett
2. *How Christians Made Peace with War* by John Driver
3. *They Loved Their Enemies* by Marian Hostetler
4. *The Good News of Justice* by Hugo Zorrilla
5. *Freedom for the Captives* by José Gallardo
6. *When Kingdoms Clash* by Calvin E. Shenk
7. *Doing What Is Right* by Lois Barrett
8. *Making War and Making Peace* by Dennis Byler
9. *A Life for a Life?* by Vernon W. Redekop
10. *Helping Resolve Conflict* by I. M. Friedmann

The books in this series are published in North America by:

Herald Press
616 Walnut Avenue
Scottdale, PA 15683
USA

Herald Press
490 Dutton Drive
Waterloo, ON N2L 6H7
CANADA

For overseas distribution or permission to translate, write to the Scottdale address listed above.